How can we start an export business from Germany in 2025?

A complete guide from company registration to export step-by-step

MD SAHID

GLOVYA EXIM

Glovya Exim is an imprint of Self-Published author Md Sahid

How can we start an export business from Germany in 2025? A complete guide from company registration to export step-by-step

For permission requests, please get in touch with the author at:

Email: mohammadsahid.star@gmail.com

Disclaimer: The information contained in this book is for general informational purposes only. However, the author assumes no responsibility or liability for any errors, omissions, or changes in applicable laws, regulations, or procedures that may occur after publication. Readers should consult with appropriate professionals for specific advice tailored to their needs.

ISBN-13: 978-93-341-9500-2

Edition: 2025

Self-Published by: MD SAHID

Contents

Preface

"How can we start an export business from Germany in 2025? A complete guide from company registration to export step-by-step" is essential for entrepreneurs and business owners looking to expand their horizons and venture into the global market. This comprehensive book provides a clear, structured pathway to help you navigate the complexities of exporting from Germany.

This guide covers all aspects of the export process, from understanding export readiness and conducting thorough market research to obtaining necessary licenses and finding reliable suppliers. Each chapter is meticulously designed to offer practical advice, detailed procedures, and helpful tips, ensuring you are well-equipped to tackle the challenges of international trade.

The book is enriched with numerous helpful website links that provide valuable resources, regulatory information, and support services. Whether you're looking to understand customs procedures, secure funding, protect intellectual property, or implement effective digital marketing strategies, you'll find the information on these pages.

MD SAHID

Introduction

Overview of Exporting from Germany

Overview In 2022, Germany was the number 4 economy in the world in terms of GDP (current US$), number 3 in total exports, number 3 in total imports, number 21 economy in terms of GDP per capita (current US$) and number 5 most complex economy according to the Economic Complexity Index (ECI).

Germany is a global economic powerhouse renowned for its high-quality products and efficient export processes. Here's an overview of key aspects of exporting from Germany:

Key Export Sectors

Machinery: Industrial machinery, machine tools, and electrical machinery.

Automotive: Cars, commercial vehicles, and automotive parts.

Chemical Products: Chemicals, pharmaceuticals, and plastics.

Electrical Equipment: Electronic components, electrical appliances, and telecommunications equipment.

Transport Equipment: Aircraft, ships, and railway vehicles.

Key Export Markets

European Union: Germany's largest export market, with countries like France, the Netherlands, and Italy being major trading partners.

United States: A significant market for German goods, particularly high-end automobiles and machinery.

China: A growing market for German exports, especially in the automotive and machinery sectors.

Growth

In August 2024, the decrease in Germany's year-by-year exports was explained primarily by a decline in exports to China (€-1.24B or -15%), the United States (€-395M or -3.03%), and Switzerland (€-348M or -6.42%), and product exports decrease in Chassis, bodies, engines, etc. for motor... (€-554M or -7.96%), Electronic devices (€-517M or -17.9%), Machinery for electricity production, and distribution (€-509M or -7.46%). In August 2024, the decrease in Germany's year-by-year imports was explained primarily by a reduction of imports from Belgium (€-1.04B or -21.3%), Ireland (€-648M or -24.9%), and Austria (€-456M or -10.7%), and product imports decrease in Basic pharmaceutical products (€-1.64B or -55.3%), Electronic devices (€-1.16B or -32.5%), and Motor cars and motor caravans (€-797M or -14.4%).

Challenges and Opportunities

Challenges:

Complex Regulations: Navigating German export regulations and international trade laws can be complex.

Global Economic Uncertainty: Economic downturns can impact export demand.

Competition: Intense competition from other exporting countries.

Logistics and Supply Chain Disruptions: Potential disruptions due to global events or logistical challenges.

Opportunities:

Strong Brand Reputation: German products are known for their quality and reliability.

Advanced Technology: Germany is a leader in technology and innovation, which can drive export growth.

Skilled Workforce: A highly trained workforce contributes to the quality and efficiency of German products.

Strong Economic Foundation: A stable economy provides a solid base for export activities.

German businesses can effectively navigate the global export market and achieve sustainable growth by understanding the key factors, challenges, and opportunities.

Benefits of Exporting from Germany

Exporting from Germany offers several distinct benefits that can significantly contribute to the growth and success of your business. Here are some key advantages:

1. Strong Economic Foundation

Stable Economy: Germany's robust and stable economy provides a secure environment for businesses to thrive.

Trade Surplus: A consistently positive trade balance reinforces Germany's status as a reliable exporter.

2. Access to Global Markets

Strategic Location: Central location in Europe facilitates easy access to both EU and non-EU markets.

Free Trade Agreements: Germany benefits from numerous EU trade agreements, reducing tariffs and trade barriers.

3. High-Quality Infrastructure

Advanced Logistics: Efficient transportation networks, including roads, railways, and ports, support smooth export operations.

Technological Innovation: State-of-the-art technology and infrastructure enhance production efficiency and export processes.

4. Strong Brand Recognition

Quality Perception: German products are globally recognized for their high quality, reliability, and innovation.

Reputation for Excellence: "Made in Germany" is a mark of excellence that can enhance the marketability of your products.

5. Government Support and Incentives

Export Promotion Programs: Various programs and initiatives by the German government and trade organizations support exporters.

Financial Assistance: Access to grants, loans, and export credits to help finance export activities.

6. Diverse Industry Base

Variety of Sectors: Germany has a diverse range of industries, including automotive, machinery, chemicals, and pharmaceuticals, providing opportunities for businesses in various sectors.

Industry Expertise: Access to highly skilled professionals and industry experts.

7. Innovation and R&D

Research and Development: A strong focus on R&D ensures continuous innovation and competitiveness in the global market.

Collaborative Opportunities: Opportunities to collaborate with research institutions and universities to develop innovative products.

8. Market Expansion Opportunities

Growth Potential: Exporting allows businesses to tap into new markets, increasing revenue and growth potential.

Diversification: Expanding into international markets helps diversify business risks and reduce dependence on the domestic market.

9. Cultural and Market Insights

Consumer Preferences: Understanding international consumer preferences and trends can lead to better product development and marketing strategies.

Cross-Cultural Experience: Exposure to different cultures and markets enriches business strategies and operations.

By leveraging these benefits, businesses can enhance their competitiveness and achieve sustainable growth in the global market.

Product Selection and Market Research

Selecting the Right Product for Export from Germany

Choosing the right product for export is crucial in building a successful international business. Here are some key factors to consider when selecting a product:

1. Product Demand and Market Potential

Market Research: Conduct thorough market research to identify countries with high demand for your product.

Consumer Preferences: Understand the specific needs and preferences of your target market.

Competitive Analysis: Analyse the competitive landscape to identify opportunities and challenges.

Import Regulations: Research import regulations, tariffs, and non-tariff barriers in your target markets.

2. Product Quality and Standards

Quality Assurance: Ensure your product meets high-quality standards to compete globally.

Certifications and Standards: Comply with relevant industry standards and certifications (e.g., CE marking for electrical products).

Packaging and Labelling: Use appropriate packaging and labelling to protect your products during transportation and meet import regulations.

3. Export Potential and Profitability

Profit Margins: Calculate the potential profit margins, considering production costs, shipping costs, customs duties, and taxes.

Export Costs: Factor in transportation, insurance, and customs fees.

Currency Exchange Rates: Consider the impact of currency exchange rate fluctuations on your profitability.

4. Product Differentiation

Unique Selling Proposition (USP): Identify what makes your product unique and desirable to international buyers.

Brand Building: Develop a strong brand identity and reputation to differentiate your products.

Innovation: Continuously innovate and improve your products to stay ahead of the competition.

5. German Product Strengths

Engineering and Technology: Germany is renowned for its high-quality engineering and technological products.

Automotive Industry: German cars and auto parts are highly sought-after globally.

Machinery and Equipment: German machinery and equipment are known for their precision and reliability.

Chemicals and Pharmaceuticals: Germany has a strong chemical and pharmaceutical industry presence.

Some popular German export products include:

Machinery and Equipment: Industrial machinery, machine tools, and electrical machinery.

Automotive Products: Cars, commercial vehicles, and automotive parts.

Chemical Products: Chemicals, pharmaceuticals, and plastics.

Electrical Equipment: Electronic components, electrical appliances, and telecommunications equipment.

Transport Equipment: Aircraft, ships, and railway vehicles.

By carefully considering these factors and selecting products with high export potential, you can increase your chances of success in the global market.

Identifying Target Markets for German Exporters

Potential Target Markets for German Exporters

While the specific target markets will vary depending on your product or service, here are some countries and regions that often present significant opportunities for German exporters:

European Union (EU): Countries like France, the Netherlands, Italy, and Poland offer significant opportunities due to geographic proximity, cultural similarities, and established trade relationships.

United States: A large and lucrative market for high-quality German products, particularly in sectors like automotive, machinery, and chemicals.

Despite geopolitical tensions, China is a significant market, especially for automotive components and industrial machinery.

India: The Indian market offers significant opportunities for German exports, particularly in machinery, electronics, and pharmaceuticals.

Other Asian Markets: Countries like Japan and South Korea offer growth potential, particularly in advanced technologies and luxury goods.

Emerging Markets: Countries in Latin America, Africa, and the Middle East, such as Brazil, Mexico, South Africa, and the United Arab Emirates, offer emerging opportunities.

Identifying Market Demand and Competition

Understanding market demand and the competitive landscape is critical to entering any foreign market successfully. By identifying areas with strong demand and assessing existing competition, you can better position your product and refine your market strategy to meet consumer needs. Here's a comprehensive guide on identifying market demand and competition for exports from Germany.

1. Conducting Demand Analysis

Start by researching global and regional demand for your product or service. Demand analysis helps you determine where consumers or businesses actively seek solutions your product offers.

Review Global Trade Data: Analysing import statistics by product category lets you see which countries bring large volumes of similar products. High import numbers indicate higher demand in that region.

Analyse Trends and Growth Projections: Use industry reports to gauge whether demand for your product is stable, growing, or declining. Emerging industries often present significant opportunities but may also have higher entry risks.

Identify Industry-Specific Demand Drivers: Different industries have unique demand factors, such as technological advancement, demographic shifts, or regulatory changes. For instance, the demand for eco-friendly products is growing worldwide due to increased environmental awareness.

Useful Resources:

Trade Map by ITC: Offers trade statistics and demand trends by product and country.

World Bank and OECD Economic Data: Provides economic indicators that affect demand, such as GDP, household income, and consumer spending.

2. Customer Needs and Preferences

Understanding target customers' preferences and purchasing behaviour is essential for identifying demand. This will help you tailor your product or marketing approach to meet customer expectations.

Consumer Surveys and Reports: Review consumer research and reports to learn about purchasing behaviour, product preferences, and price sensitivity.

Social Media and Search Trends: Platforms like Google Trends and social media analytics can offer insights into what people are searching for, which reflects current demand and interest levels.

Customer Demographics: Analyse factors such as age, income, location, and lifestyle, as these influence purchasing power and preferences. For instance, younger demographics might favour digital products, while older groups prefer tangible goods.

Useful Tools:

Google Trends: Helps gauge popular search topics by country, which can indicate demand patterns.

Statista: Provides statistics and reports on consumer behaviour and industry trends across markets.

3. Assessing Competitive Landscape

Understanding the competition in each market allows you to evaluate the ease or difficulty of entering that market. This step also helps you identify potential market gaps your product can fill.

Identify Key Competitors: List competitors already established in your target markets. Look for both local businesses and international companies with a presence there.

Evaluate Competitor Strengths and Weaknesses: Study competitors' market share, pricing strategies, product features, and customer reviews to understand what makes them successful. This analysis can also highlight areas where your product might have a competitive edge.

Analyse Market Saturation: Determine whether the market is saturated or has room for new entrants. Highly saturated markets require a strong differentiation strategy, while underserved markets may offer opportunities for quicker growth.

Useful Tools:

Euromonitor International: Provides detailed competitor and market analyses across global industries.

Crunchable: Offers insights into companies, including competitor information, to gauge market presence and investment levels.

4. Pricing and Positioning in the Competitive Landscape

Pricing is critical in competitive positioning, particularly in markets with established players. Analysing competitor pricing and positioning can help you set a competitive but profitable price point.

Benchmark Competitor Pricing: Review competitors' pricing structures in your target market. Adjusting prices to reflect market expectations while maintaining profitability is essential.

Identify Unique Selling Points (USPs): Determine the unique features, quality standards, or brand values that differentiate your product from the competition. For example, if competitors prioritize low prices, positioning your product as a premium, high-quality alternative can appeal to a different market segment.

Consider Bundling or Added Value: Sometimes, adding value through bundles, extended warranties, or additional services can set your product apart in a crowded market.

5. Market Entry Barriers and Competitive Risks

Understand the challenges or barriers to entry in your target market and anticipate potential competitive responses. Identifying these factors early can help refine your market strategy and risk assessment.

Market Entry Challenges: These may include high tariffs, regulatory restrictions, or complex logistics. Some competitors might already have local partnerships that give them logistical or pricing advantages.

Risk of New Entrants: Some markets are more prone to new competitors, especially if they offer low entry barriers. Consider markets where you have a strong advantage or where unique product aspects reduce the likelihood of quick imitation.

Competitive Response: Established companies in a market might respond to new entrants with price cuts, increased marketing, or loyalty programs. Understanding potential responses will help you plan your entry strategy.

Useful Resources:

PWC's Doing Business Guides: These guides provide insights into business challenges by country, including competition and regulatory barriers.

Export.gov Country Commercial Guides: These guides include competitive environment analysis and information on business regulations.

6. Testing Demand with Pilot Exports

Testing the market by starting with small-scale exports or launching a pilot project can help gauge real-world demand without significant financial risk.

Run a Pilot Program: Begin with a limited product launch or distribution in a target market. This lets you collect customer feedback, monitor sales, and identify areas for improvement.

Participate in Trade Fairs: Trade fairs allow you to showcase your product to a broad audience, assess interest levels, and network with potential customers and distributors.

Online and E-commerce Channels: For consumer products, testing demand through online sales platforms like Amazon, eBay,

Regional e-commerce sites can provide valuable insights with relatively low investment.

Summary

Identifying market demand and assessing competition involves combining data analysis, competitor research, and real-world testing. Using available tools, analysing customer behaviour, and understanding competitive positioning will help you decide which markets to enter and how to differentiate your product. By following these steps, German exporters can pinpoint markets with solid demand and navigate the competitive landscape effectively, maximizing their chances for success.

Understanding Export Regulations

Foreign Trade and Payments Act (Außenwirtschaftsgesetz - AWG)

The Foreign Trade and Payments Act (AWG) is Germany's primary legislation governing foreign trade, mainly focused on maintaining the country's economic stability, security, and adherence to international obligations. The AWG lays the groundwork for regulating imports, exports, and foreign transactions, ensuring they align with German and European Union (EU) policies. It's vital for German companies engaging in international trade and foreign investments, as it defines how goods, services, and capital can cross borders.

Key Objectives of the AWG

The AWG's main objectives include:

Safeguarding Security and Public Order: Ensuring that exports and foreign investments do not threaten Germany's security, particularly sensitive technologies, military goods, and strategic sectors.

Compliance with International Obligations: Germany, as a member of the EU and other international organizations, must adhere to trade policies that support global stability and non-proliferation of weapons.

Promoting Economic Stability: Managing the impact of foreign trade on the domestic economy, including protecting German industries and technologies from harmful foreign control or influence.

Compliance and Licensing Under the AWG

Businesses engaging in export activities or foreign transactions subject to AWG restrictions must apply for licenses or approvals through relevant authorities:

Federal Office for Economic Affairs and Export Control (BAFA): BAFA is the main body overseeing export controls, reviewing license applications for exporting controlled goods, and ensuring compliance with AWG regulations.

Federal Ministry for Economic Affairs and Climate Action (BMWK): BMWK handles foreign investment reviews and grants approvals or imposes restrictions when necessary.

Businesses must conduct thorough internal audits to assess if their goods or services fall under the AWG's control. Non-compliance with AWG can result in significant penalties, including fines and restrictions on future trade operations.

EU Dual-Use Regulation

The EU Dual-Use Regulation (Regulation (EU) 2021/821) is a comprehensive legal framework that governs the control of exports, brokering, technical assistance, transit, and transfer of dual-use.

Items. These items are goods, software, and technology that can be used for civilian and military purposes.

Key Points of the EU Dual-Use Regulation:

Control of Dual-Use Items: The regulation aims to prevent the proliferation of weapons of mass destruction and to protect national security.

Export Licenses: In many cases, exporting dual-use items requires a license from the relevant national authorities.

Brokering and Technical Assistance: Controls are also in place for brokering and providing technical assistance related to dual-use items.

Intra-EU Transfers: While most dual-use items can be freely transferred within the EU, certain sensitive items may require prior authorization.

International Cooperation: The EU cooperates with other countries and international organizations to ensure adequate export controls.

Key Implications for Businesses

Due Diligence: Businesses must conduct due diligence on their customers and end-users to ensure that items are not diverted for unauthorized purposes.

Record-Keeping: Accurate and detailed records of all transactions related to dual-use items must be kept.

Compliance with Sanctions: Businesses must comply with EU and international sanctions regimes.

Export Controls Officer: Larger companies may need to appoint a dedicated export controls officer to oversee compliance.

Firearms Regulation

Germany has strict gun control laws designed to prioritize public safety. Here's a brief overview:

Key Regulations:

Weapons Act (Waffengesetz): This is the primary legislation governing firearms and ammunition in Germany. It outlines the types of weapons permitted, licensing requirements, storage regulations, and restrictions on ownership and use.

European Firearms Directive: Germany adheres to this EU directive, which sets minimum standards for acquiring and possessing firearms across member states.

Embargo Regulations

Embargoes are government-imposed restrictions on trade with specific countries or entities. They are often used as a political tool to pressure target countries into changing their behaviour. Embargoes can be broad, restricting all trade, or targeted, focusing on specific goods or services.

Common Reasons for Embargos

Political Reasons: To protest a country's policies or actions.

Human Rights Violations: To pressure a country to improve its rights record.

Security Concerns: To limit the flow of goods that could be used for military or terrorist purposes.

Economic Sanctions: To weaken a country's economy and force it to comply with demands.

Key Implications of Embargos

Trade Restrictions: Embargos limit or prohibit importing and exporting goods and services.

Economic Impact: Embargoes can have significant financial consequences, affecting industries, jobs, and overall economic growth.

Geopolitical Tensions: Embargos can escalate country tensions and further political and economic conflicts.

Humanitarian Concerns: Embargos can have unintended humanitarian consequences, mainly when they restrict the flow of essential goods like food and medicine.

Choosing a Business Structure

Sole Proprietorship

A sole proprietorship is the simplest form of business ownership. It's a business owned and operated by one person. There's no legal distinction between the owner and the business itself.

Key Characteristics of a Sole Proprietorship:

Easy to Start: Minimal legal formalities are required to set up a sole proprietorship.

Complete Control: The owner has full control over all aspects of the business.

Unlimited Liability: The owner is liable for all business debts and obligations.

Taxation: Profits are taxed as personal income.

Limited Access to Capital: Raising capital can be challenging compared to other business structures.

Advantages of a Sole Proprietorship

Simplicity: Easy to set up and manage.

Flexibility: The owner has complete control over business decisions.

Minimal Legal Formalities: Fewer regulatory requirements compared to other structures.

Tax Benefits: Profits are taxed as personal income, which can be advantageous.

Disadvantages of a Sole Proprietorship

Unlimited Liability: The owner's assets are at risk.

Limited Capital: Raising capital can be difficult.

Lack of Continuity: The business may cease if the owner becomes incapacitated or dies.

Limited Growth Potential: The owner's resources and capabilities may limit the business's growth.

Steps to Set Up a Sole Proprietorship:

Choose a Business Name: Ensure it's unique and compliant with local naming regulations.

Register Your Business: Register with relevant local or state authorities.

Obtain Necessary Licenses and Permits: Depending on your industry, you may need specific licenses or permits.

Open a Business Bank Account: Keep personal and business finances separate.

Set Up Accounting: Implement a financial management system and track income and expenses.

When to Choose a Sole Proprietorship

A sole proprietorship is often a good choice for small businesses with low start-up costs and limited risk. It's suitable for individuals who want to be their boss and have complete control over their business.

Partnership

A **partnership** involves two or more individuals sharing ownership, responsibilities, and profits. This structure can be beneficial for businesses that need diverse skills and resources. Here are the details:

Key Features:

Shared Ownership: Two or more partners own and operate the business.

Joint Decision-Making: Partners collaborate on business decisions and share responsibilities.

Profit Sharing: Profits are divided among partners based on the partnership agreement.

Personal Liability: Partners are personally liable for business debts and obligations unless they form a limited partnership.

Types of Partnerships:

General Partnership:

Equal Responsibility: All partners are equally responsible for management and debts.

Liability: Partners have unlimited personal liability.

Limited Partnership:

General and Limited Partners: Includes both general partners (who manage the business and have unlimited liability) and limited partners (who invest but have limited liability).

Liability: Limited partners are only liable up to their investment.

Limited Liability Partnership (LLP):

Limited Liability: Partners have limited personal liability for business debts.

Management: Partners share management duties and have protection against personal liability for the actions of other partners.

Advantages:

Combined Resources: Pooling of financial resources, skills, and expertise.

Shared Responsibilities: Responsibilities and workload are shared among partners.

Flexibility: Flexible management structure compared to corporations.

Disadvantages:

Joint Liability: Partners are jointly and severally liable for business debts (except in LLPs).

Potential Conflicts: Disagreements between partners can affect business operations.

Profit Sharing: Profits must be shared among partners, which can lead to disputes.

Ideal for:

Businesses that benefit from diverse skills, knowledge, and capital contributions from multiple individuals.

Steps to Set Up a Partnership:

Choose Partners: Select partners with complementary skills and a shared vision.

Draft a Partnership Agreement: Outline roles, responsibilities, profit-sharing ratios, dispute resolution, and exit strategies.

Register the Partnership: Register with local or state authorities and obtain necessary licenses and permits.

Obtain an EIN: Apply for an Employer Identification Number (EIN) from the IRS.

Open a Business Bank Account: Keep personal and business finances separate.

Set Up Accounting: Implement an accounting system to manage finances and track income and expenses.

When to Choose a Partnership

A partnership can be a good option for businesses that require significant capital investment, specialized skills, or shared risk. Considering the potential benefits and drawbacks before forming a partnership is essential.

Limited Liability Company (LLC)

A **Limited Liability Company (LLC)** combines the liability protection of a corporation with the tax benefits and flexibility of a partnership. Here's a detailed look at its features, advantages, and considerations:

Key Features:

Limited Liability: Owners (members) are not personally liable for business debts and liabilities.

Flexibility: Offers flexibility in management and organization.

Separate Legal Entity: An LLC is a separate legal entity from its owners, protecting personal assets.

Pass-Through Taxation: Profits and losses can be passed to the owners' income without corporate taxes.

Advantages:

Liability Protection: Members have limited personal liability for business debts.

Tax Benefits: Pass-through taxation avoids double taxation; LLCs can be taxed as a corporation.

Management Flexibility: Can be managed by members or appointed managers.

Operational Simplicity: Fewer formalities and requirements compared to a corporation.

Disadvantages:

Limited Life: In some jurisdictions, the LLC may dissolve if a member leaves unless specified otherwise in the operating agreement.

Self-Employment Taxes: Members may need to pay self-employment taxes on their share of profits.

Complexity in Formation: It is more complex and costly to set up than sole proprietorships or partnerships.

Ideal for:

Small to medium-sized businesses seeking liability protection with flexible management and tax options.

Steps to Set Up an LLC:

Choose a Name: Select a unique name that complies with state regulations and includes "LLC" in the title.

File Articles of Organization: Submit the articles of organization to your state's business filing office.

Create an Operating Agreement: Draft an operating agreement outlining the management structure, roles, responsibilities, and distribution of profits.

Obtain an EIN: Apply for an Employer Identification Number (EIN) from the IRS for tax purposes.

Register for State Taxes: Depending on your state, you may need to register for state taxes.

Obtain Necessary Permits and Licenses: Ensure you have all required permits and licenses to operate legally.

Open a Business Bank Account: Separate your personal and business finances by opening a business bank account.

Comply with Ongoing Requirements: Stay compliant with state requirements, including annual reports and fees.

When to Choose an LLC:

An LLC is suitable for many businesses, especially small and medium-sized enterprises. It's particularly beneficial for companies that:

Want limited liability protection

Desire pass-through taxation

Require flexibility in management and ownership structure

Need to attract investors or partners

It's essential to consult with a legal professional to understand the rules and regulations governing LLCs in your jurisdiction and ensure proper formation and compliance.

Corporation

A **corporation** is a legal entity separate from its owners, providing the highest level of liability protection and potential for growth. Here's an in-depth look at its features, advantages, and considerations:

Key Features:

Separate Legal Entity: A corporation is legally distinct from its owners (shareholders), offering protection for personal assets.

Ownership through Shares: Ownership is divided into shares of stock, which can be bought and sold.

Perpetual Existence: A corporation exists even if ownership changes or shareholders leave.

Complex Structure: Requires a board of directors and officers and adherence to formalities and regulations.

Advantages:

Limited Liability: Shareholders are not personally liable for business debts beyond their investment in the corporation.

Access to Capital: Ability to raise capital through the sale of stock.

Credibility: Corporations often have greater credibility with customers, suppliers, and lenders.

Tax Benefits: Potential for lower overall tax rates and additional tax benefits.

Disadvantages:

Complexity and Cost: More complex and expensive to set up and maintain than other business structures.

Double Taxation: Corporate profits may be taxed at the corporate and shareholder levels (dividends).

Regulatory Requirements: Subject to more regulatory requirements, including annual reports and shareholder meetings.

Types of Corporations:

C Corporation (C Corp):

Standard Corporation: Unlimited number of shareholders and no restrictions on ownership.

Double Taxation: Profits are taxed at the corporate level, and dividends are taxed at the shareholder level.

S Corporation (S Corp):

Pass-Through Taxation: Profits and losses pass through to shareholders' tax returns, avoiding double taxation.

Ownership Restrictions: Limited to 100 shareholders.

Eligibility: Must meet specific eligibility criteria to elect S Corp status.

Non-Profit Corporation:

Purpose: Organized for charitable, educational, religious, or other non-profit purposes.

Tax-Exempt Status: May qualify for tax-exempt status under IRS guidelines.

Restrictions: Prohibited from distributing profits to shareholders; profits must be reinvested in the organization's mission.

Ideal for:

Businesses looking to raise significant capital, operate on a large scale, or benefit from limited liability and perpetual existence.

Steps to Set Up a Corporation:

Choose a Business Name: Ensure the name is unique and complies with state regulations.

File Articles of Incorporation: Submit the articles of incorporation to your state's business filing office.

Create Corporate Bylaws: Draft bylaws that outline the governance and management structure of the corporation.

Appoint Directors and Officers: Appoint a board of directors and corporate officers to manage the corporation.

Obtain an EIN: Apply for an Employer Identification Number (EIN) from the IRS for tax purposes.

Register for State Taxes: Depending on your state, you may need to register for state taxes.

Issue Stock: Issue shares of stock to initial shareholders.

Hold Organizational Meeting: Conduct an organizational meeting to approve bylaws, appoint officers, and address other initial matters.

Obtain Necessary Permits and Licenses: Ensure you have all required permits and licenses to operate legally.

Comply with Ongoing Requirements: Stay compliant with state and federal requirements, including annual reports and shareholder meetings.

When to Choose a corporation:

A corporation is suitable for businesses that:

Require significant capital investment

Want to attract investors

Need a long-term, stable structure

Desire limited liability protection

It's essential to consult with a legal professional to determine the most appropriate corporate structure for your business and to ensure compliance with all legal and regulatory requirements.

Cooperative

A **cooperative** is a business structure where the enterprise is owned and operated by a group of individuals for their mutual benefit. Here's a detailed look at its features, advantages, and considerations:

Key Features:

Member-Owned: The cooperative is owned and controlled by its members, who use its products or services.

Democratic Governance: Each member typically has one vote, regardless of the number of shares owned.

Profit Distribution: Profits are distributed among members based on participation rather than investment size.

Limited Liability: Members have limited liability, protecting personal assets.

Advantages:

Shared Resources: Pooling resources among members can lead to better purchasing power and shared benefits.

Member Control: Members have a direct say in the business operations and decision-making.

Profit Sharing: Members share the profits, which can lead to increased loyalty and motivation.

Tax Benefits: Cooperatives may receive favourable tax treatment, such as exemptions or reduced tax rates.

Disadvantages:

Complex Setup: Establishing a cooperative can be more complicated and time-consuming than other business structures.

Decision-Making Challenges: Democratic governance can sometimes lead to slower decision-making processes.

Capital Limitations: Raising capital can be challenging, as cooperatives cannot issue stock like corporations.

Dependency on Member Participation: The success of a cooperative often relies heavily on active member participation and commitment.

Types of Cooperatives:

Consumer Cooperatives: Owned by the consumers who buy the goods and services.

Producer Cooperatives: Owned by producers of commodities or crafts who have joined forces to process and market their products.

Worker Cooperatives: Owned and operated by the employees of the business.

Housing Cooperatives: Owned by residents who share the benefits and responsibilities of homeownership.

Financial Cooperatives: Credit unions provide financial services to their members.

Ideal for:

Groups of individuals or businesses with everyday needs or goals, such as farmers, artisans, retailers, or residents looking for shared services or purchasing power.

Steps to Set Up a Cooperative:

Gather a Group of Founders: Identify a group with a shared interest in forming a cooperative.

Conduct a Feasibility Study: Assess the viability of the cooperative, including market analysis and financial projections.

Draft Bylaws and Business Plan: Create bylaws that outline the cooperative's structure, governance, and operational rules, along with a comprehensive business plan.

Register the Cooperative: File the necessary documents with your state or country's business registration office.

Raise Capital: Collect initial capital from member contributions or seek funding from cooperative-friendly financial institutions.

Hold Organizational Meeting: Elect a board of directors and appoint officers as per the bylaws.

Obtain Necessary Permits and Licenses: Ensure the cooperative has all required permits and licenses to operate legally.

Open a Business Bank Account: Separate personal and cooperative finances by opening a business bank account.

Begin Operations: Start providing services or products to members and begin business operations.

Opening a Business Bank Account

Choosing the Right Bank

Choosing the right bank for your export business in Germany is crucial for smooth operations and financial efficiency. Here are some top banks that cater to export businesses in Germany:

Top Banks for Export Businesses in Germany:

Commerzbank: Known for its strong support for international trade, it offers comprehensive trade finance services, including letters of credit, bank guarantees, and export credit. They have a robust global network and provide advisory services tailored for SMEs.

Deutsche Bank: Offers a wide range of international banking services, including trade finance, foreign exchange, and global payment solutions. They have a strong presence in key trade corridors.

N26: A digital-first bank that provides robust online and mobile banking services, making it easy to manage export transactions. They offer competitive Forex rates and support for international payments.

Qonto: A digital business bank that combines banking services with invoicing and bookkeeping tools. They offer credit and loan options, making it a comprehensive solution for SMEs.

Wise Business: Known for its low-cost international money transfers and transparent fees, it is a good option for export businesses.

Key Considerations:

Trade Finance Services: Look for banks that offer comprehensive trade finance services like Letters of Credit, bank guarantees, and export credit.

Foreign Exchange (Forex) Rates: Choose a bank with competitive Forex rates and hedging options to manage currency risk.

Global Network: Opt for banks with a strong global network of correspondent banks to facilitate international transactions.

Customer Support: Ensure the bank provides dedicated support for exporters, including trade specialists and advisory services.

Digital Banking: Consider banks that offer robust online and mobile banking platforms for easy management of export transactions.

You can ensure smooth and efficient financial operations by considering these factors and choosing a bank that aligns with your export business needs.

Required Documents

When opening a business bank account, you must gather several key documents to verify your business and identity. Here's a list of commonly required documents:

1. Proof of Identity

Valid Government-Issued ID: Passport, driver's license, or national ID card for all signatories.

2. Business Registration Documents

Articles of Incorporation or Formation: Official documents that establish your business as a legal entity (for corporations or LLCs).

Partnership Agreement: A partnership agreement if you're operating as a partnership.

Business License: The local government issues your business license or permit.

Fictitious Business Name (FBN) Statement: If you operate under a trade name.

3. Proof of Business Address

Utility Bills: Recent utility bills in the business's name.

Lease Agreement: A lease agreement for your business premises.

Rental Agreement: Rental agreement if you rent your business space.

4. Tax Identification Number (TIN)

Employer Identification Number (EIN): Issued by the IRS for tax purposes.

Social Security Number (SSN): For sole proprietors without an EIN.

5. Operating Agreement or Bylaws

Operating Agreement: For LLCs, outlining the management structure and operating procedures.

Corporate Bylaws: For corporations, detailing the governance structure and rules.

6. Beneficial Ownership Information

Ownership Details: Information on individuals who own or control a significant portion of the business.

7. Other Relevant Documents

Partnership Resolutions: For partnerships, authorize the opening of the bank account.

Minutes of Meetings: Minutes from board or member meetings authorizing the account opening (for corporations or LLCs).

Additional Tips

Bank-Specific Requirements: Check with your chosen bank for any specific additional requirements or forms.

Documentation Updates: Ensure all documents are current and reflect your business details accurately.

Obtaining Necessary Licenses and Permits

Export Licenses

An export license in Germany is mandatory if your business plans to export controlled items, such as dual-use goods (items with both civilian and military applications), military equipment, or goods to sanctioned destinations. **BAFA** (Federal Office for Economic Affairs and Export Control) is the primary authority overseeing export licenses.

Steps to Obtain an Export License:

Determine Export Control Status:

Check if German or EU export control laws regulate your products. BAFA's website offers guidance and access to the **Export Control Classification Number (ECCN)**.

Register with BAFA:

Create an account on BAFA's **ELAN-K2 online portal** to manage your application and document submission.

ELAN-K2 Portal

Prepare Documentation:

Key documents include product details, end-user certificates, and related contracts or purchase orders.

Submit and Wait for Approval:

Processing times vary, but sensitive items may take weeks or months to approve. BAFA will notify you of the approval or any additional requirements.

Ongoing Compliance:

Track and monitor exported goods to ensure they are used as declared. This helps prevent diversion to unauthorized uses or destinations.

Customs License

A customs license enables your business to manage customs procedures for exporting goods outside the EU. **German Customs (Zoll)** oversees these licenses and the overall customs process. Most exporters in Germany need an **EORI (Economic Operators Registration and Identification) Number**, which is essential for interacting with EU customs authorities.

Steps to Obtain a Customs License and EORI Number:

Register for an EORI Number:

Apply for an EORI number through the German customs portal. This identifier is crucial for all customs declarations and interactions with customs offices in Germany and across the EU.

EORI Registration

Apply for AEO Certification (Optional):

If your business plans to frequently export goods, consider **Authorized Economic Operator (AEO) certification** for simplified customs procedures. This certification, while optional,

Offers benefits like faster customs processing and reduced inspections.

Set Up a Customs Compliance Program:

Compliance programs can help ensure adherence to customs regulations. This includes employee training, record-keeping of exports, and regular audits to reduce potential delays or penalties.

Customs Declarations and Documentation:

Each export must be documented and declared at customs. Commonly required documents include invoices, packing lists, and export licenses (if applicable). Customs agents can assist with filing, and companies can file electronically using the **ATLAS** system.

VAT Registration for Export Businesses

VAT (Value-Added Tax) registration is necessary for most businesses in Germany. However, exports are usually exempt from VAT because goods sold outside the EU are classified as zero-rated for VAT. Nevertheless, registration is essential to maintain compliance and allows you to reclaim VAT on business expenses in Germany.

Steps to Register for VAT:

Register with the German Tax Office (Finanzamt):

New businesses must register with the **Finanzamt** to obtain a **Steuernummer** (tax number) and **VAT ID (USt-IdNr)**. This ID is essential for invoicing and tax filing.

File VAT Returns:

Although exports are zero-rated, VAT returns must be filed periodically, detailing domestic and international transactions. You must also retain proof that the goods were exported, such as shipping records or customs documents.

VAT Reclaim on Purchases:

VAT incurred on business expenses within Germany can often be reclaimed, reducing the overall cost of doing business.

Intrastat Reporting:

If exporting goods within the EU, businesses may need to submit **Intrastat declarations** to report the movement of goods for statistical purposes.

Summary

Starting an export business in Germany involves several key regulatory steps:

Export License from BAFA for controlled or sensitive goods.

Customs License and **EORI Number** for all goods exported outside the EU, with optional AEO certification for streamlining.

VAT Registration to ensure compliance with German tax regulations, even though exports are zero-rated.

By securing the proper licenses and permits, your business can legally and efficiently export products from Germany, reducing delays and ensuring compliance with international trade laws.

Finding Reliable Suppliers and Manufacturers

Sourcing Products Locally

Sourcing products locally in Germany can be a great way to ensure quality and support local businesses. Here are some steps and tips to help you find reliable local suppliers:

Steps to Source Products Locally:

Identify Your Needs: Clearly define your needed products, including specifications, quantities, and delivery timelines.

Research Local Suppliers: Use online directories, business directories, and industry-specific databases to find local suppliers. Websites like Alibaba, ThomasNet, and Global Sources can also be helpful.

Attend Local Trade Shows and Exhibitions: Participate in industry-specific trade shows and exhibitions to meet potential suppliers in person.

Network with Industry Professionals: Connect with other businesses in your industry to get recommendations and referrals.

Contact Manufacturers Directly: Reach out to manufacturers to discuss your needs and evaluate their capabilities.

Evaluate Supplier Credentials: Check for certifications, quality control measures, and customer reviews. Look for suppliers with

ISO certifications, quality management systems, and positive feedback.

Request Samples and Quotes: Ask for product samples and detailed quotes to assess the quality and pricing of the products.

Conduct Site Visits: If possible, visit the supplier's facilities to inspect their operations and ensure they meet your standards.

Negotiate Terms and Conditions: Discuss payment terms, delivery schedules, and other important terms to ensure a clear and mutually beneficial agreement.

Tips for Finding Reliable Local Suppliers:

Start with a Shortlist: Begin with a small list of potential suppliers and gradually narrow it down based on your evaluations.

Use Technology: Utilize online tools and platforms for supplier discovery and management.

Build Long-Term Relationships: Focus on long-term partnerships with suppliers for consistent quality and reliability.

Stay Updated: Keep an eye on industry trends and changes to ensure your suppliers remain competitive and reliable.

By following these steps and tips, you can find reliable local suppliers in Germany that will help your export business thrive.

Building Strong Supplier Relationships

Building strong supplier relationships is essential for maintaining a reliable and efficient supply chain. Here are some strategies to help you establish and nurture these relationships:

1. Clear Communication

Open Dialogue: Maintain regular and transparent communication with your suppliers. Discuss expectations, requirements, and any potential issues upfront.

Feedback Loop: Provide constructive feedback and be open to receiving it from your suppliers. This helps in mutual improvement and promptly addresses concerns.

2. Mutual Respect and Trust

Trust Building: Establish trust by being honest and reliable. Deliver on your promises and expect the same from your suppliers.

Fair Treatment: Treat your suppliers as partners rather than just vendors. Recognize their contributions and show appreciation.

3. Long-Term Commitment

Partnership Mindset: Focus on long-term collaboration rather than short-term gains. Building a lasting relationship can lead to better terms, loyalty, and performance.

Joint Planning: Involve suppliers in planning and decision-making processes. This fosters a sense of partnership and mutual benefit.

4. Performance Metrics

Set Clear Expectations: Define and agree on key performance indicators (KPIs) to measure the supplier's performance.

Regular Reviews: Conduct regular performance reviews and provide feedback. Recognize good performance and address any areas of concern.

5. Collaborative Problem Solving

Joint Problem Solving: Work with your suppliers to find solutions when issues arise. This collaborative approach can strengthen the relationship and lead to better outcomes.

Flexibility: Be flexible and understanding when suppliers face challenges. Support them in finding solutions rather than immediately seeking alternatives.

6. Technology Integration

Use Technology: Implement solutions that facilitate seamless communication, order management, and performance tracking.

Data Sharing: Share relevant data and insights with your suppliers to help them improve their processes and better meet your needs.

7. Fair Negotiation

Win-Win Negotiation: Approach negotiations to achieve mutually beneficial agreements. Avoid putting undue pressure on suppliers, which can harm the relationship.

Transparent Pricing: Be transparent about pricing and cost structures. This builds trust and helps negotiate fair terms.

8. Risk Management

Diversify Suppliers: Avoid over-reliance on a single supplier by diversifying your supplier base. This reduces risk and ensures continuity.

Contingency Planning: Develop contingency plans for supply chain disruptions. Work with suppliers to identify potential risks and mitigation strategies.

By focusing on these strategies, you can build strong, reliable, mutually beneficial relationships with your suppliers.

Export Documentation and Logistics

Export Documentation

Export documentation is essential for shipping goods from Germany to other countries, ensuring legal compliance, and facilitating customs clearance. Proper documentation minimizes delays, meets international standards, and provides key information about exported products. Here are the core documents often required for exporting from Germany:

1. Commercial Invoice

The **Commercial Invoice** is a critical document in any export shipment as it serves as a contract and proof of sale between the seller and the buyer. It provides essential details about the transaction, including:

Exporter and Importer Information: Name, address, and contact information of both parties.

Invoice Number and Date: Unique identifier for record-keeping and traceability.

Description of Goods: Detailed information about the shipped goods, including quantity, unit price, and total price.

HS Code: Harmonized System Code classifies the products for customs purposes, affecting duties and taxes.

Terms of Sale and Payment: Information on payment terms (e.g., incoterms like FOB, CIF) and agreed payment methods.

Currency: Currency in which the payment will be made.

Total Invoice Value: Total cost of goods, including applicable charges or discounts.

Purpose: The Commercial Invoice is used by customs authorities to assess duties and taxes and is required for customs clearance. It also serves as an essential accounting document for both parties.

2. Packing List

The **Packing List** provides a detailed breakdown of the shipment's contents, which is essential for customs and logistical purposes. Unlike the Commercial Invoice, the Packing List focuses on packaging details.

Key details included in a Packing List:

Exporter and Importer Information: Contact information for both the exporter and importer.

Packing List Number and Date: Reference number for tracking.

Contents of Each Package: Detailed list of goods in each package, including descriptions, weights, dimensions, and quantity.

Package Identification: Identifying numbers or marks on each package for easy identification.

Weight and Volume: Gross and net weight of each package and overall shipment volume.

Purpose: Customs authorities use the Packing List to verify the shipment contents, aiding inspection and handling. It's also used by the receiving party to check the shipment on arrival, ensuring all goods are accounted for.

3. Bill of Lading (BOL)

The **Bill of Lading** is a legally binding document issued by the carrier (e.g., shipping line) to the exporter. It serves as both a receipt for the goods and a contract for transportation, confirming that the goods have been received and outlining the terms of transport.

Key components of a Bill of Lading:

Exporter, Importer, and Carrier Information: Details of all parties involved in the shipment.

Description of Goods: Includes shipment quantities, weight, and dimensions.

Shipping Instructions: Specifies the route, mode of transportation, and destination.

Terms of Delivery and Payment: Incoterms and payment terms, including responsibility for costs and risks.

Signature: Carrier's signature, certifying receipt of goods.

Types of Bill of Lading:

Straight BOL: Goods delivered directly to the consignee.

Order BOL: Can be transferred by endorsement, often used in transactions involving payment through banks.

Purpose: The Bill of Lading serves as proof of shipment, a title document, and a receipt for goods. It's crucial for claiming goods at the destination and is required by banks for payment processing in international transactions.

4. Certificate of Origin (COO)

The **Certificate of Origin** is an official document certifying the origin of the goods being exported. It is often issued by a Chamber of Commerce or relevant government authority in Germany. It certifies that the goods are produced, manufactured, or processed in a specific country (Germany, in this case).

Key details in a Certificate of Origin:

Exporter and Importer Information: Contact information for both parties.

Description of Goods: Including product names, quantities, and values.

Origin Declaration: Certification that the goods originated from Germany.

Certification Authority Stamp and Signature: Issued and stamped by an authorized body, like the German Chamber of Commerce.

Purpose: The COO is used by customs authorities to determine if goods qualify for preferential tariff rates under trade agreements. It's also essential to meet import regulations in the destination country, especially in countries with strict origin requirements.

5. Inspection Certificates

An inspection certificate is a document that verifies the quality, quantity, and conformity of goods to specific standards or specifications. In Germany, various organizations issue inspection certificates for different products and industries.

Common Types of Inspection Certificates in Germany

TÜV Certificate:

Issued by organizations like TÜV SÜD and TÜV Rheinland.

Verifies the safety and quality of products, particularly in the automotive, industrial, and consumer goods sectors.

Often required for importing goods into certain countries.

GS Mark:

Stands for "Geprüfte Sicherheit" (Tested Safety).

Certifies that a product meets German safety standards.

Commonly used for electrical and electronic products.

CE Marking:

Indicates that a product complies with EU health, safety, and environmental requirements.

It is mandatory for many products sold within the EU.

Food Safety Certificates:

Issued by organizations like the German Federal Institute for Risk Assessment (BfR).

Certifies that food products meet hygiene and safety standards.

Material Test Certificates:

Issued by testing laboratories to verify the properties of materials.

It is commonly used in the construction, automotive, and aerospace industries.

How to Obtain an Inspection Certificate?

Identify the Required Certificate: Determine the specific certificate needed for your product and the target market.

Select a Certification Body: Choose a reputable certification body accredited to issue the required certificate.

Prepare Documentation: Gather all necessary documentation, such as product specifications, technical drawings, and test reports.

Undergo Inspection: The certification body will conduct inspections to verify product quality and compliance with standards.

Issue of Certificate: The certification body will issue the certificate upon inspection completion.

Importance of Inspection Certificates

Ensuring Quality: Inspection certificates assure product quality and safety.

Facilitating Import and Export: They can help streamline customs clearance and reduce delays.

Building Trust with Customers: They demonstrate a commitment to quality and compliance.

Meeting Regulatory Requirements: They help businesses comply with national and international regulations.

By obtaining appropriate inspection certificates, German exporters can enhance their credibility and facilitate smooth international trade.

Having accurate and complete export documentation is essential for smooth customs processing and compliance with international trade regulations.

Choosing the Right Shipping Method

Selecting the optimal shipping method is crucial for efficient and cost-effective international shipping. Here's a breakdown of the primary options:

1. Sea Freight

Best for: Large shipments, low-value goods, and non-urgent deliveries.

Pros: Cost-effective for large quantities, suitable for heavy and bulky items.

Cons: Longer transit times than air freight, the potential for delays due to port congestion.

2. Air Freight

Best for: High-value, time-sensitive, or perishable goods.

Pros: Faster delivery times, suitable for urgent shipments.

Cons: More expensive than sea freight, limited cargo capacity.

3. Courier Services

Best for Small packages, documents, and urgent shipments.

Pros: Door-to-door delivery, tracking capabilities, and additional services like customs clearance.

Cons: More expensive than sea or air freight for larger shipments.

Factors to Consider When Choosing a Shipping Method:

Product Value: High-value items may benefit from faster, more secure air freight.

Delivery Time: Urgent shipments may require air freight, while less time-sensitive goods can be shipped by sea.

Shipment Size and Weight: The size and weight of your shipment will influence the most cost-effective method.

Product Sensitivity: Perishable or fragile goods may require specialized handling and temperature-controlled shipping.

Budget: Consider the cost of each shipping method and balance it with delivery time and insurance needs.

Additional Tips:

Choose a Reliable Shipping Partner: Select a reputable shipping company with experience in international shipping.

Proper Packaging: Ensure your goods are securely packaged to withstand the rigors of transportation.

Precise and Accurate Documentation: Prepare all necessary customs documents to avoid delays and penalties.

Insurance: Consider purchasing adequate insurance coverage to protect your shipment against loss or damage.

Track Your Shipment: Use tracking services to monitor the progress of your shipment.

By carefully considering these factors and selecting the appropriate shipping method, you can ensure that your goods reach their destination safely, efficiently, and cost-effectively.

Customs Procedures and Regulations

Harmonized System (HS) Codes

The Harmonized System (HS) is an internationally standardized system of names and numbers for classifying traded products. It's crucial for customs clearance and tariff calculations.

Importance of HS Codes: Correctly classifying your goods using HS codes ensures accurate customs valuations, duty rates, and tariff preferences.

Impact on Duties and Taxes: HS codes determine the applicable customs duties and taxes on your goods.

Verification and Validation: Customs authorities may verify the accuracy of HS codes, so it's essential to consult with customs experts or use specialized software.

Customs Duties and Taxes

Import Duties: Taxes levied on imported goods.

Export Duties: Taxes levied on exported goods (less common).

Value-Added Tax (VAT): A consumption tax added to the price of goods and services.

Other Taxes: Specific taxes may apply to certain goods; such as excise duties or environmental taxes.

Customs Clearance Procedures

Customs clearance is the process of inspecting and releasing imported or exported goods. The specific procedures can vary depending on the country and the type of goods being imported or exported.

General Steps Involved in Customs Clearance:

Document Submission: Submit all required customs documents, including the commercial invoice, packing list, bill of lading, and certificate of origin.

Customs Inspection: Customs authorities may inspect the goods to verify their classification and value.

Duty and Tax Payment: Pay any applicable customs duties and taxes.

Customs Clearance Release: Once all requirements are met, customs authorities will rclease the goods for delivery.

Insurance for Export Shipments

Insurance is essential to protect your goods during transit. Consider the following types of insurance:

Marine Cargo Insurance: Covers losses or damage to goods during transportation by sea or inland waterways.

Air Cargo Insurance: Covers losses or damage to goods during air transportation.

All-Risk Insurance: Provides comprehensive coverage against various risks, including loss, damage, theft, and natural disasters.

Key Considerations for German Exporters:

EU Trade Agreements: Germany benefits from various free trade agreements within the EU, which can reduce or eliminate tariffs on exports to other EU member states.

Export Controls: Certain goods, particularly dual-use items, may require specific export licenses from the German authorities.

Customs Procedures: Familiarize yourself with German customs procedures and regulations to ensure smooth clearance of your exports.

Logistics and Shipping: Choose a reliable logistics provider to handle your goods' transportation and customs clearance.

By understanding these key aspects of customs procedures and regulations, you can ensure smooth and efficient international shipping. It's always advisable to consult with a customs broker or freight forwarder to navigate the complexities of customs clearance and minimize potential delays and costs.

Payment, Price Quotation Methods, and Currency Exchange

When exporting from Germany, choosing secure and efficient payment methods is crucial to mitigate risks and ensure timely payments. Here are some standard payment methods and currency exchange considerations:

Secure Payment Methods

Letter of Credit (L/C):

A secure payment method where a bank guarantees payment to the exporter.

Protects the exporter from buyer default.

It can be complex and time-consuming.

Telegraphic Transfer (TT):

A direct transfer of funds from the buyer's bank to the exporter's bank.

It is faster than L/Cs but offers less protection.

Documentary Collection (D/C):

A hybrid method where the exporter ships the goods and presents documents to the buyer's bank for payment.

It offers less security than L/Cs but is simpler and faster.

Advance Payment:

The buyer pays in advance before the goods are shipped.

It offers the most security for the exporter but can be risky for the buyer.

Price Quotation Methods

When exporting from Germany, quoting prices accurately and effectively is crucial. Here are some standard pricing methods:

1. Ex-Works (EXW):

Seller's Responsibility: The seller makes the goods available at their premises.

Buyer's Responsibility: The buyer bears all costs and risks associated with transportation, insurance, and customs clearance.

Best for: Experienced importers who can manage the entire shipping process.

2. Free Carrier (FCA):

Seller's Responsibility: The seller is responsible for delivering the goods to a specified carrier at a named place.

Buyer's Responsibility: The buyer is responsible for export clearance, transportation, and insurance.

Best for: When the buyer has a preferred carrier or wants to manage the shipping process.

3. Free Alongside Ship (FAS):

Seller's Responsibility: The seller is responsible for delivering the goods alongside the ship at a named port of shipment.

Buyer's Responsibility: The buyer is responsible for loading the goods onto the ship and subsequent transportation.

Best for: When the buyer arranges for ocean shipping.

4. Cost, Insurance, and Freight (CIF):

Seller's Responsibility: The seller is responsible for arranging transportation, insurance, and customs clearance to the designated destination port.

Buyer's Responsibility: The buyer is responsible for importing the goods and paying import duties and taxes.

Best for: When the buyer wants a simple and all-inclusive price.

5. Cost and Freight (CFR):

Seller's Responsibility: The seller arranges transportation to the destination port.

Buyer's Responsibility: The buyer is responsible for insurance and customs clearance.

Best for: When the buyer wants to arrange insurance and customs clearance.

Factors to Consider When Quoting Prices:

Currency: Determine the currency in which you will quote your prices.

Payment Terms: Specify the payment terms, such as letter of credit, telegraphic transfer, or documentary collection.

Shipping Costs: Calculate the estimated shipping costs, including freight charges, insurance, and customs duties.

Exchange Rate Fluctuations: Consider the potential impact of currency exchange rate fluctuations.

Import Duties and Taxes: Research the import duties and taxes that may apply in the buyer's country.

Profit Margins: Ensure that your pricing strategy allows for adequate profit margins.

Additional Tips for Effective Quotation:

Clear and Concise: Present your quotations clearly and concisely.

Detailed Specifications: Provide detailed specifications of your products or services.

Include Terms and Conditions: Clearly outline the terms and conditions of the sale.

Offer Flexible Payment Options: Consider offering different payment terms to accommodate buyer preferences.

Be Responsive: Respond promptly to inquiries and requests for information.

Understanding these pricing methods and factors allows you to develop effective pricing strategies and build strong relationships with your international customers.

Currency Exchange

Foreign Exchange Risk: Fluctuations in exchange rates can impact the profitability of export transactions.

Hedging Techniques: Exporters can use hedging techniques like forward contracts, options, and futures to manage currency risk.

Currency Exchange Services: Utilize the services of banks or specialized foreign exchange brokers to exchange currencies at competitive rates.

Key Considerations:

Risk Assessment: Evaluate the buyer's creditworthiness and choose a payment method with appropriate protection.

Payment Terms: Negotiate favourable payment terms, such as a combination of advance payment and a letter of credit.

Currency Risk Management: Implement effective currency risk management strategies to minimize losses.

Bank Relationship: Maintain a strong relationship with your bank to access specialized services and expert advice.

Consult with Experts: Seek advice from international trade experts or a financial advisor to optimize your payment strategies.

By carefully considering these factors and choosing appropriate payment methods and currency exchange strategies, German exporters can minimize risks and ensure timely payments.

Marketing and Sales Strategies

Digital Marketing for International Markets

Digital marketing has revolutionized the way businesses reach global audiences. Here are some key strategies to effectively market your products or services internationally:

1. Search Engine Marketing (SEM)

Pay-Per-Click (PPC) Advertising:

Target specific keywords and demographics to reach potential customers.

Use platforms like Google Ads to create targeted ad campaigns.

Utilize ad extensions to provide additional information and improve click-through rates.

Search Engine Optimization (SEO):

Optimize your website's content and structure for search engines.

Use relevant keywords and phrases to improve search engine rankings.

Build high-quality backlinks to increase website authority.

2. Social Media Advertising

Platform Selection: Choose platforms relevant to your target audience, such as Facebook, Instagram, LinkedIn, and Twitter.

Social Media Platforms

Targeted Advertising: Use demographic, interest, and behavioural targeting to reach specific audience segments.

Engaging Content: Create high-quality, visually appealing content that resonates with your target audience.

Influencer Marketing: Collaborate with influencers to reach a wider audience and build brand credibility.

3. Content Marketing

Blogging: Create informative and engaging blog posts to attract and retain visitors to your website.

Video Marketing: Produce high-quality videos to showcase your products or services and explain complex concepts.

Email Marketing: Build an email list and send targeted email campaigns to nurture leads and drive conversions.

Content Localization: Adapt your content to different cultures and languages to resonate with your target audience.

Additional Tips for International Digital Marketing

Cultural Sensitivity: Understand cultural nuances and tailor your marketing messages accordingly.

Language Localization: Translate your website and marketing materials into relevant languages.

Local SEO: Optimize your website for local search engines in your target markets.

International Shipping and Logistics: Ensure efficient and cost-effective shipping to your customers.

Payment Methods: Offer various payment options to cater to international customers.

Customer Support: Provide excellent customer support in multiple languages.

Analytics and Tracking: Use analytics tools to monitor the performance of your international marketing campaigns.

By effectively implementing these digital marketing strategies, you can reach a global audience, increase brand awareness, and drive sales for your German export business.

Building Relationships with International Importers

Building strong relationships with international importers is crucial for the success of your export business. Here are some effective strategies:

1. Trade Fairs and Exhibitions

Identify Relevant Fairs: Research and participate in industry-specific trade fairs and exhibitions in your target markets.

Pre-Event Preparation: Create a comprehensive list of potential buyers and schedule in-person meetings.

Effective Networking: Actively network with potential importers, exchange business cards, and follow up promptly.

Professional Presentation: Prepare a compelling presentation highlighting your products or services, their unique selling points, and your company's capabilities.

Post-Event Follow-up: Send personalized follow-up emails or calls to maintain contact and nurture relationships.

2. Business Networking

Industry Associations: Join relevant associations to connect with other businesses and potential importers.

Online Networking Platforms: Utilize platforms like LinkedIn to connect with professionals in your target markets.

Business Delegations: Participate in government-led trade delegations to network with potential buyers and government officials.

Chambers of Commerce: Leverage the resources and networks of local and international chambers of commerce.

3. Appointment Setting

Targeted Outreach: Identify potential importers and contact them directly through email, phone, or social media.

Personalized Approach: Tailor your outreach messages to each importer's needs and interests.

Clear Value Proposition: Highlight your products or services' unique benefits and value.

Persistence and Follow-up: Be persistent in your follow-up efforts, but avoid being overly aggressive.

Effective Communication: Use clear and concise communication, and bc prepared to answer questions and address concerns.

Additional Tips:

Cultural Sensitivity: Understand and respect the cultural nuances of your target markets.

Language Proficiency: Have a good command of the language of your target market or use translation services.

Build Trust: Establish trust by being reliable, transparent, and ethical in your business dealings.

Offer Excellent Customer Service: Provide timely and effective customer support to build long-term relationships.

Adapt to Local Market Needs: Be willing to adapt your products or services to meet the specific needs of your target market.

By implementing these strategies and building strong relationships with international importers, you can increase your export sales and expand your global market reach.

Effective Sales Techniques and Negotiation Skills

Mastering effective sales techniques and negotiation skills can significantly impact your business success. Here are some key strategies to consider:

Effective Sales Techniques

Understanding Customer Needs: Listen actively to your customers to understand their needs, preferences, and pain points. Tailor your sales pitch to address these aspects.

Building Relationships: Focus on building long-term relationships rather than making a one-time sale. Trust and rapport are crucial for customer loyalty.

Product Knowledge: Be knowledgeable about your product or service. This enables you to answer questions confidently and highlight the benefits and features that matter most to the customer.

Value Proposition: Clearly articulate the unique value your product or service offers. Explain how it solves the customer's problem or improves their situation.

Storytelling: Use storytelling to make your sales pitch more engaging. Share success stories or case studies demonstrating your product's positive impact.

Handling Objections: Be prepared to handle objections calmly and effectively. Listen to the customer's concerns, acknowledge them, and provide solutions or alternatives.

Closing Techniques: Develop various closing techniques, such as the assumptive close, the urgency close, and the summary close, to help secure the sale.

Negotiation Skills

Preparation: Do thorough research before entering any negotiation. Understand the other party's needs, preferences, and constraints.

Set Clear Goals: Define your objectives and know your bottom line. Understand what you are willing to compromise on and what is non-negotiable.

Build Rapport: Establish a positive relationship with the other party. Building trust and rapport can lead to more successful negotiations.

Active Listening: Pay attention to what the other party is saying. Active listening helps you understand their needs and respond appropriately.

Win-Win Approach: Aim for a win-win outcome where both parties feel satisfied with the agreement. This approach fosters long-term relationships and trust.

Effective Communication: Communicate clearly and assertively. Be confident but not aggressive. Ensure that your points are understood and that you understand the other party's points.

Flexibility: Be open to alternatives and compromises. Flexibility can help you find creative solutions that satisfy both parties.

Manage Emotions: Keep your emotions in check during negotiations. Stay calm and composed, even in challenging situations.

By implementing these sales techniques and negotiation skills, you can enhance your ability to close deals and build strong, lasting business relationships.

Legal and Tax Implications

Tax Implications for Export Businesses

VAT and Export VAT Refunds

Value-added tax (VAT) is a consumption tax added to the price of goods and services. While VAT is generally applicable to sales within the EU, it can have implications for export businesses:

Zero-Rating: Exported goods and services are typically zero-rated, meaning VAT is not charged.

Input Tax Recovery: Businesses can claim VAT paid on goods and services used in producing or supplying exported goods. This is known as input tax recovery.

To claim VAT refunds, businesses must:

Register for VAT: Ensure your business is registered for VAT in the EU country where it is established.

Keep Accurate Records: Maintain detailed records of all transactions, including invoices, receipts, and customs documentation.

Submit VAT Returns: File timely VAT returns to claim input tax credits.

Comply with Customs Procedures: Ensure that your export shipments comply with customs regulations to facilitate VAT refunds.

Corporate Taxes

Corporate tax rates vary across EU countries. However, there are several tax incentives and benefits available to export-oriented businesses:

Reduced Corporate Tax Rates: Some countries offer reduced corporate tax rates for export-oriented businesses.

Tax Deductions: Certain expenses related to export activities, such as marketing, research and development, and international transportation, may be tax-deductible.

Tax Credits: Some countries provide tax credits for export-related activities, such as R&D or investment in export infrastructure.

Double Taxation Agreements: These agreements help reduce or eliminate double taxation on income earned from cross-border activities.

It's important to note that tax laws and regulations can be complex and subject to change. It's advisable to consult with a tax advisor or accountant to ensure compliance and maximize tax benefits.

Key Considerations for German Exporters:

German VAT: Understand the specific VAT rules and regulations in Germany, including the threshold for VAT registration and the procedures for claiming VAT refunds.

Intra-EU Trade: Use a valid VAT identification number to take advantage of the VAT exemption for intra-EU trade.

International Tax Treaties: Germany has numerous double taxation treaties with other countries, which can help reduce your tax burden.

Consult with a Tax Advisor: Seek professional advice to optimize your tax strategy and ensure compliance with all relevant regulations.

By understanding the tax implications of exporting from Germany and taking advantage of available tax benefits, businesses can improve their profitability and competitiveness in the global market.

Intellectual Property Rights Protection

Protecting your intellectual property (IP) is crucial when exporting from Germany. Here's a breakdown of the key IP rights and how to protect them:

1. Trademark Registration

A trademark is a distinctive sign that identifies the origin of goods or services. In Germany, trademarks can be registered with the German Patent and Trade Mark Office (DPMA).

Key points to consider:

Types of Trademarks: Word marks, figurative marks, and combination marks.

Registration Process: Involves filing an application, conducting a search, and potentially facing opposition proceedings.

Protection Scope: Protects against unauthorized use of the trademark.

2. Patent Registration

A patent grants exclusive rights to an invention for a limited period. In Germany, patents can be registered with the DPMA or the European Patent Office (EPO).

Key points to consider:

Types of Patents: Utility models (for simpler inventions) and patents (for more complex inventions).

Patenting Process: Involves filing an application, undergoing examination, and potentially facing opposition proceedings.

Protection Scope: Protects the invention from unauthorized use, manufacture, or sale.

3. Copyright Protection

Copyright protects original works of authorship, such as literary, artistic, and musical works. In Germany, copyright protection arises automatically upon creation.

Key points to consider:

No Formal Registration Required: Copyright protection is automatic.

Protection Scope: Protects the expression of ideas, not the ideas themselves.

Enforcement: Copyright holders can take legal action to enforce their rights.

Additional Considerations

Design Rights: Protect the aesthetic appearance of products.

Trade Secrets: Confidential business information can be protected through trade secret laws.

Tips for Protecting Your IP in Germany:

Consult with an IP Attorney: Seek advice from an experienced IP attorney to understand the specific requirements and complexities of IP protection in Germany.

Register Your IP: Register your trademarks, patents, and designs to obtain legal protection.

Monitor for Infringement: Regularly monitor the market for potential infringements of your IP rights.

Take Action Against Infringement: If you suspect infringement, take immediate legal action to protect your rights.

International Protection: Consider international registration options to protect your IP rights in multiple countries.

By understanding and protecting your intellectual property rights, you can safeguard your business interests and maintain a competitive edge in the global market.

Contractual Agreements and Dispute Resolution

International Contract Law

International contracts are agreements between parties from different jurisdictions. When drafting international contracts, it's crucial to consider the following:

Choice of Law: Specify the governing law to determine the interpretation and enforcement of the contract.

Dispute Resolution: Choose a suitable dispute resolution mechanism, such as arbitration or litigation.

Force Majeure: Include a force majeure clause to address unforeseen circumstances like natural disasters or political unrest.

Confidentiality: Protect sensitive information through confidentiality clauses.

Intellectual Property Rights: Clearly define IP rights and ownership.

Payment Terms: Specify payment terms, currencies, and any applicable taxes.

Delivery Terms: Clearly outline delivery terms, including shipping methods, insurance, and risk transfer.

Dispute Resolution Mechanisms

Negotiation: A voluntary process where parties attempt to reach a mutually agreeable solution.

Mediation: A neutral third party helps facilitate communication between the involved parties and assists them in settling.

Arbitration: A formal process where a neutral arbitrator decides the dispute.

Litigation: A legal process involving courts to resolve disputes.

Choosing the Right Dispute Resolution Mechanism:

Consider the following factors when selecting a dispute resolution mechanism:

Cost: Arbitration and mediation are often less expensive than litigation.

Time: Arbitration and mediation can be faster than litigation.

Confidentiality: Arbitration and mediation can be more confidential than litigation.

Enforceability: Ensure the chosen mechanism is enforceable in the relevant jurisdictions.

Expertise: Select a neutral party with expertise in the subject matter.

Tips for Effective International Contract Negotiation:

Prepare Thoroughly: Research your counterparty and understand their needs and priorities.

Active Listening: Pay attention to the other party's perspective and ask clarifying questions.

Clear Communication: Use clear and concise language to avoid misunderstandings.

Flexibility: Be open to compromise and creative solutions.

Build Trust: Develop strong relationships with your international partners.

By understanding international contract law and effectively managing disputes, you can mitigate risks and ensure the smooth execution of your export business.

Finance Management and Funding

Securing Funding for Your Export Business

Bank Loans

Traditional Bank Loans: Secure loans from commercial banks to finance working capital, inventory, or capital expenditures.

Export Credit Financing: Specialized loans banks offer to support export activities, often backed by export credit agencies.

Letter of Credit: A bank guarantee issued by a buyer's bank to ensure payment to the exporter.

Government Grants and Subsidies

Export Credit Agencies: Government agencies that provide financial support to exporters, such as export credit insurance, loans, and guarantees.

Regional Development Funds: Regional development funds may offer grants or subsidies to businesses in specific regions.

Small Business Grants: Government programs that provide financial assistance to small businesses, including exporters.

Venture Capital

Venture Capital Firms: Invest in high-growth potential businesses in exchange for equity.

Angel Investors: Individual investors who provide capital to early-stage companies.

Additional Funding Options

Crowdfunding: Raise funds from a large number of individuals through online platforms.

Family and Friends: Seek funding from family and friends who believe in your business idea.

Bootstrapping: Self-funding your business by reinvesting profits or using personal savings.

Key Considerations for Securing Funding:

Business Plan: A well-prepared business plan is essential to attract investors.

Financial Projections: Accurate financial projections, including cash flow forecasts, are crucial.

Collateral: Be prepared to offer collateral, such as property or equipment, to secure loans.

Strong Management Team: A strong and experienced management team can increase your chances of securing funding.

Clear Value Proposition: Articulate your unique value proposition to potential investors.

Track Record: A strong track record of success can enhance your credibility.

Network and Build Relationships: Network with potential investors and industry experts.

By carefully considering these funding options and taking proactive steps to secure financing, you can fuel the growth of your export business.

Managing Cash Flow and Inventory

Adequate cash flow and inventory management are crucial for the success of any export business, including those based in Germany. Here are some key strategies to consider:

Cash Flow Management

1. Accurate Forecasting:

Utilize historical data and market trends to predict future cash inflows and outflows.

Consider factors like seasonal variations, economic cycles, and potential disruptions.

2. Timely Invoicing and Payments:

Implement efficient invoicing procedures to ensure timely payments from customers.

Offer flexible payment options, such as credit cards or online payment gateways.

Consider using a factoring service to accelerate cash flow.

3. Efficient Accounts Receivable Management:

Monitor outstanding invoices closely and follow up promptly.

Consider using debt collection services for overdue payments.

4. Managing Working Capital:

Optimize inventory levels to minimize holding costs.

Negotiate favourable payment terms with suppliers.

Monitor cash conversion cycles to improve efficiency.

Inventory Management

1. Demand Forecasting:

Use historical data, market trends, and industry forecasts to predict future demand.

Consider factors like seasonal variations, economic conditions, and promotional activities.

2. Inventory Optimization:

Implement a robust inventory management system to track stock levels, monitor reorder points, and optimize inventory turnover.

Utilize techniques like just-in-time (JIT) inventory or vendor-managed inventory (VMI) to minimize holding costs.

Consider using warehouse management systems (WMS) to streamline inventory processes.

3. Quality Control:

Establish strict quality control procedures to ensure product quality and consistency.

Implement regular quality checks and inspections.

Work closely with suppliers to maintain high-quality standards.

4. Risk Management:

Identify potential risks, such as supply chain disruptions, natural disasters, or political instability.

Develop contingency plans to mitigate these risks.

Diversify your supply chain to reduce reliance on a single supplier or shipping route.

By effectively managing cash flow and inventory, you can improve your business's financial health, reduce costs, and enhance customer satisfaction.

Conclusion

Future Trends in the German Export Market

E-commerce and Digital Trade

Online Marketplaces: German exporters can leverage global e-commerce platforms like Amazon, eBay, and Alibaba to reach a wider international audience.

Cross-Border E-commerce: Expanding into cross-border e-commerce will allow German businesses to tap into new markets and reach consumers directly.

Digital Marketing: Utilizing digital marketing tools like SEO, SEM, and social media can help businesses attract international customers.

Payment Solutions: Offering various payment options, including digital wallets and mobile payments, can enhance the customer experience.

Sustainability and Green Technologies

Green Products and Services: Focusing on sustainable and environmentally friendly products can attract eco-conscious consumers.

Circular Economy: Adopting circular economy principles can reduce waste, conserve resources, and improve brand reputation.

Renewable Energy Technologies: Germany is a leader in renewable energy technology, offering significant export opportunities.

Green Supply Chains: Building sustainable supply chains can help reduce environmental impact and improve brand image.

Other Emerging Trends:

Industry 4.0: Embracing digital technologies to improve manufacturing processes, increase efficiency, and enhance product quality.

Artificial Intelligence and Machine Learning: Utilizing AI and ML to optimize operations, personalize customer experiences, and develop innovative products.

Blockchain Technology: Leveraging blockchain to secure supply chains, track product provenance, and facilitate transparent transactions.

By staying informed about these trends and adapting to the changing global landscape, German exporters can maintain their competitive edge and thrive in the international market.

Recap

Market Research: Identify target markets, analyse market potential, and understand local regulations.

Business Structure: Choose a suitable legal structure (e.g., GmbH, AG, sole proprietorship).

Export License: Obtain necessary licenses, especially for dual-use goods or restricted items.

Customs Clearance: Prepare required documentation (commercial invoice, packing list, bill of lading, certificate of origin) and comply with customs regulations.

Logistics and Shipping: Select a reliable logistics provider and choose the appropriate shipping method (sea, air, or courier).

Payment Methods: Consider secure payment methods like letters of credit, telegraphic transfers, or documentary collections.

Insurance: Protect your shipments with adequate insurance coverage.

Marketing and Sales: Develop effective marketing and sales strategies, including digital marketing, trade fairs, and building relationships with importers.

Useful Websites and References

https://www.bafa.de/EN/Foreign_Trade/Export_Control/export_control_node.html

https://www.gtai.de/en/invest

https://www.bmwk.de/Redaktion/EN/Dossier/export-initiatives.html

https://www.dihk.de/en

https://www.zoll.de/EN/Businesses/Movement-of-goods/Export/export_node.html

https://trade.ec.europa.eu/access-to-markets/en/content/welcome-access2markets-market-access-database-users

https://ec.europa.eu/taxation_customs/dds2/taric/taric_consultation.jsp

https://www.gesetze-im-internet.de/englisch_awg/englisch_awg.html

https://www.intracen.org/

https://trade.ec.europa.eu/

https://www.wto.org/

https://marketfinder.thinkwithgoogle.com/intl/en_in

https://www.trademap.org/Index.aspx

https://www.euromonitor.com/

https://www.statista.com/

https://www.handelsregister.de/rp_web/welcome.xhtml

https://www.allianz-trade.com/en_global.html

How can we start an export business from Germany in 2025?

https://iccwbo.org/

https://www.wcoomd.org/

https://oec.world/en/profile/country/deu?redirect=true

https://exportimportpractical.com/choose-products-export/

https://www.commerzbank.com/corporateclients/about-us/export-bank/

https://www.monito.com/en/wiki/best-business-bank-account-germany

https://blackthorneit.com/blog/how-to-obtain-an-export-license-in-germany-your-simple-guide/

https://www.lawyersgermany.com/special-licenses-and-permits-in-germany

https://www.vat-germany.com/blog/introduction-to-vat-registration-in-germany-for-global-companies/

https://globalriskcommunity.com/profiles/blogs/transforming-your-company-with-operational-resilience

https://templatesz234.com/marketing-competitor-analysis-templates-for-market-intelligence/

https://importersecurityfile.com/commercial-invoice-isf-filing-terms-definitions-explained/2/

https://www.truelanguage.com/manufacturing-leverage-language-services-to-boost-international-sales/

www.ingramcontent.com/pod-product-compliance
Ingram Content Group UK Ltd.
Pitfield, Milton Keynes, MK11 3LW, UK
UKHW011513190726
13845UKWH00034B/1237

9 789334 195002